AN APPEAL FOR SELF-SUPPORTING LABORERS TO ENTER UNWORKED FIELDS

A CALL TO FINISH THE WORK

AN
E. G. WHITE COMPILATION

Copyright © 2017 TEACH Services, Inc.
Copyright © 2017 Adventist-Laymen's Services & Industries
ISBN-13: 978-1-4796-0846-1 (Paperback)
Library of Congress Control Number: 2017910873

This title has been published in cooperation with Adventist-Laymen's Services & Industries, Harbert Hills Academy and TEACH Services, Inc.

This book was originally published in 1930 as a call to Adventist laymen to take up the work of the three angels of Revelation 14 and proclaim the gospel and the second coming to every nation, tongue, kindred and people.

– Steve Dickman, ASI President

TEACH Services, Inc.
PUBLISHING
www.TEACHServices.com • (800) 367-1844

Table of Contents

Introduction

Sound an Alarm

Sound an alarm throughout the length and breadth of the earth. Tell the people that the day of the Lord is near, and hasteth greatly. Let none be left unwarned. We might have been in the place of the poor souls that are in error. We might have been placed among barbarians. According to the truth we have received above others, we are debtors to impart the same to them.[1]

Behold a Perishing World

We are on the verge of the eternal world. The judgments of God are already begun to fall upon the inhabitants of the land. God sends these judgments to bring men and women to their senses. He has a purpose in everything that He permits to take place in our world, and He desires us to be so spiritually-minded that we shall be able to perceive His work in the events so unusual in the past, but now of almost daily occurrence.

We have before us a great work—the closing work of giving God's last warning message to a sinful world. But what have we done to give this message? Look, I beg of you, at the many, many places that have never yet been even entered. Look at our workers treading over and over the same ground, while around them is a neglected world, lying in wickedness and corruption, — a world as yet unwarned. To me this is an awful picture. What appalling indifference we manifest to the needs of a perishing world![2]

---

[1] *Testimonies for the Church*, vol. 6, p. 22
[2] *Testimonies for the Church*, vol. 7, p. 103

1

The Call of the Hour

The Last Crisis

We are living in the time of the end. The fast-fulfilling signs of the times declare that the coming of Christ is near at hand. The days in which we live are solemn and important. The Spirit of God is gradually but surely being withdrawn from the earth. Plagues and judgments are already falling upon the despisers of the grace of God. The calamities by land and sea, the unsettled state of society, the alarms of war, are portentous. They forecast approaching events of the greatest magnitude.

The agencies of evil are combining their forces, and consolidating. They are strengthening for the last great crisis. Great changes are soon to take place in our world, and the final movements will be rapid ones.[3]

Labor While Probation Lingers

The judgments of God are in the earth, and, under the influence of the Holy Spirit, we must give the message of warning that He has entrusted to us. We must give this message quickly, line upon line, precept upon precept. Men will soon be forced to great decisions, and it is our duty to see that they are given an opportunity to understand the truth, that they may take their stand intelligently on the right side. The Lord calls upon His people to labor—labor earnestly and wisely—while probation lingers.[4]

The Church to Arouse

Upon us rests the weighty responsibility of warning the world of its coming doom. From every direction, from far and near, are coming

---

[3] *Testimonies for the Church*, vol. 9, p. 11
[4] *Testimonies for the Church*, vol. 9, pp. 126, 127

calls for help. God calls upon His church to arise, and clothe herself with power. Immortal crowns are to be won; the kingdom of heaven is to be gained; the world, perishing in ignorance, is to be enlightened.[5]

Earnest Work to be Done

There is stern, earnest work to be done. The pioneers in our work put forth untiring effort. Let all now take hold and act as if they were preparing for a great harvest. Let them go forth to work with the Bible in their hands, and may the Lord give them a true, peaceable spirit. I beseech our church members not to lose precious time in confusing and hindering the work of the Lord.[6]

Encouraging One Another

God's servants are to make use of every resource for enlarging His kingdom. The apostle Paul declares that it is "good and acceptable in the sight of God our Saviour; who will have all men to be saved, and to come into the knowledge of the truth," that "supplications, prayers, intercessions, and giving of thanks, be made for all men." 1 Timothy 2:3, 4, 1. And James says, "Let him know, that he which converteth the sinner from the error of his way shall save a soul from death, and shall hide a multitude of sins." James 5:20. Every believer is pledged to unite with his brethren in giving the invitation, "Come; for all things are now ready." Luke 14:17. Each is to encourage the others in doing whole-hearted work. Earnest invitations will be given by a living church. Thirsty souls will be led to the water of life.[7]

Fierce Opposition

It is as true now as when Christ was upon earth that every inroad made by the gospel upon the enemy's dominion is met by fierce opposition from his vast armies. The conflict that is right upon us will be the most terrible ever witnessed. But though Satan is represented as being as strong as the strong man armed, his overthrow will be complete, and every one who unites with him in choosing apostasy rather than loyalty will perish with him.[8]

---

[5] *Testimonies for the Church*, vol. 7, p. 16
[6] *Australasia Union Conference Record,* March 18, 1907
[7] *Manuscript 127-1901*, November 26, 1901
[8] *Testimonies for the Church*, vol. 6, p. 407

Without Wavering

We are in no wise to be deterred from fulfilling our commission by the listlessness, the dullness, the lack of spiritual perception in those upon whom the word of God is brought to bear. We are to preach the word of life to those whom we may judge to be as hopeless subjects as though they were in their graves. Though they may seem to be unwilling to hear or to receive the light of truth, without questioning or wavering, we are to do our part.[9]

Wake Up

Let the gospel message ring through our churches, summoning them to universal action. Let the members of the church have increased faith, gaining zeal from their unseen, heavenly allies, from a knowledge of their exhaustless resources, from the greatness of the enterprise in which they are engaged, and from the power of their Leader. Those who place themselves under God's control, to be led and guided by Him, will catch the steady tread of the events ordained by Him to take place. Inspired with the Spirit of Him who gave His life for the life of the world, they will no longer stand still in impotency, pointing to what they cannot do. Putting on the armor of heaven, they will go forth to the warfare, willing to do and dare for God, knowing that His omnipotence will supply their need.[10]

As agents for Jesus Christ men are to be laborers together with God. Why then are so many acting as did Meroz, doing nothing, while those sitting in darkness receive no light, no help from those who claim to be the children of God? How much do such idlers resemble the angel who is represented as flying in the midst of heaven, proclaiming the commandments of God and the faith of Jesus? Christ is saying to these idlers in the market place, "Go work today in my vineyard."[11]

---

[9] *The Review and Herald*, January 17, 1893
[10] *Testimonies for the Church*, vol. 7, p. 14
[11] *The Southern Worker*, October 10, 1899

2

What the Church Can Do

Convincing Power

The world will be convinced, not by what the pulpit teaches, but by what the church lives. The minister in the desk announces the theory of the gospel; the practical piety of the church demonstrates its power.[12]

The Church an Angel of Light

We have no time to waste. God has provided a means of recovery for sinners. By unselfish work His truth is to be represented. This is the trust He has given us, and it is to be faithfully executed.

When will the church do her appointed work? She is represented as an angel of light, flying through heaven with the everlasting gospel to be proclaimed to the world. This represents the speed and directness with which the church is to prosecute her work. In the medical missionary work Jesus is to behold the travail of His soul. Human beings are to be snatched as brands from the burning.[13]

Unite our Efforts

The work of God in this earth can never be finished until the men and women comprising our church membership rally to the work, and unite their efforts with those of ministers and church officers.[14]

Development of Talent in the Churches

In every church there is talent, which, with the right kind of labor, might be developed to become a great help in this work. That which is needed now for the upbuilding of our churches is the nice work of wise

---

[12] *Testimonies for the Church,* vol. 7, p. 16
[13] *Medical Ministry,* p. 131
[14] *Testimonies for the Church,* vol. 9, p. 117

laborers to discern and develop talent in the church, — talent that can be educated for the Master's use. There should be a well-organized plan for the employment of workers to go into all our churches, large and small, to instruct the members how to labor for the upbuilding of the church, and also for unbelievers. It is training, education, that is needed. Those who labor in visiting the churches should give the brethren and sisters instruction in practical methods of doing missionary work.[15]

All the preaching in the world will not make men feel deeply the need of the perishing souls around them. Nothing will so arouse in men and women a self-sacrificing zeal as to send them forth into new fields to work for those in darkness. Prepare workers to go out into the highways and hedges. Do not call men and women to the great center, encouraging them to leave churches that need their aid. Men must learn to bear responsibilities. Not one in a hundred among us is doing anything beyond engaging in common, worldly enterprises. We are not half awake to the worth of the souls for whom Christ died.[16]

We are bought him the price of Christ's own life, — bought that we may return to God His own in faithful service. We have no time now to give our energies and talents to worldly enterprises. Shall we become absorbed in serving the world, serving ourselves, and lose eternal life and the everlasting bliss of heaven? O, we can not afford to do this! Let every talent be employed in the work of God.[17]

A Call for Greater Effort

Every addition to the church should be one more agency for the carrying out of the plan of redemption. Every power of God's people should be devoted to bringing many sons and daughters to Him. In our service there is to be no indifference, no selfishness. Any departure from self-denial, any relaxation of earnest effort, means so much power given to the enemy.[18]

---

[15] *Testimonies for the Church*, vol. 9, p. 117
[16] *Testimonies for the Church*, vol. 8, pp. 147, 148
[17] *Testimonies for the Church*, vol. 9, p. 104
[18] *Testimonies for the Church*, vol. 7, p. 222

The Simplest Modes of Work

The very simplest modes of work should be devised, and set in operation among the churches. If members will co-operate with such a plan, and perseveringly carry it out, they will reap a rich reward, for their experience will grow brighter, their ability will increase through exercise, and souls will be saved through their efforts.[19]

Formation of Small Companies

Why do not believers feel a deeper, more earnest concern for those who are out of Christ? Why do not two or three meet together and plead with God for the salvation of some special one, and then for still another? In our churches let companies be formed for service. Let different ones unite in labor as fishers of men. Let them seek to gather souls from the corruption of the world into the saving purity of Christ's love.

The formation of small companies as a basis of Christian effort has been presented to me by One who cannot err. If there is a large number in the church, let the members be formed into small companies, to work not only for the church-members, but for unbelievers. If in one place there are only two or three who know the truth, let them form themselves into a band of workers. Let them keep their bond of union unbroken, pressing together in love and unity, encouraging one another to advance, each gaining courage and strength from the assistance of the others.[20]

Holding Small Meetings

Those who know not the truth should be prayed with and instructed. Many can take up this work. Small meetings should now be arranged for, in which two or three workers unite in explaining the truth to the people. Such meetings have been held in many places, and as a result, people have been brought into the truth, and meeting-houses have been built. At first, the work may have to be carried on in a room in a private house. Perhaps, if the weather is favorable, the meeting can be held out-of-doors. Give a kindly welcome to all who come. Draw near to God and to one another. Let songs of praise be sung. Let the Word

---

[19] *Testimonies for the Church*, vol. 6, p. 433
[20] *Testimonies for the Church*, vol. 7, pp. 21, 22

of God be simply and clearly explained. Such a service will make a lasting impression.[21]

Humble Laborers

There are men who never gave a discourse in their lives, who ought to be laboring to save souls. Neither great talents nor high position is required. But there is urgent need of men and women who are acquainted with Jesus, and familiar with the story of His life and death....[22]

Workers from the Ranks

Those whom God chooses as workers are not always talented in the estimation of the world. Sometimes He selects unlearned men. To these He gives a special work. They reach a class to whom others could not obtain access. Opening the heart to the truth, they are made wise in and through Christ. Their lives inhale and exhale the fragrance of godliness. Their words are thoughtfully considered before they are spoken. They strive to promote the well-being of their fellow-men. They take relief and happiness to the needy and distressed. They realize the necessity of ever remaining under Christ's training, that they may work in harmony with God's will. They study how best to follow the Saviour's example of cross-bearing and self-denial. They are God's witnesses, revealing His compassion and love, and ascribing all the glory to Him whom they love and serve.

Constantly they are learning of the great Teacher, and constantly they reach higher degrees of excellence, yet all the time feeling a sense of their weakness and inefficiency. They are drawn upward by their strong, loving admiration for Christ. They practice His virtues; for their life is assimilated to His. Ever they move onward and upward, a blessing to the world and an honor to their Redeemer. Of them Christ says, "Blessed are the meek; for they shall inherit the earth." Matthew 5:5.

Such workers are to be encouraged. Their work is done, not to be seen of men, but to glorify God. And it will bear His inspection. The Lord brings these workers into connection with those of more marked

---

[21] *Letter 66-1902*, April 24, 1902
[22] *Life Sketches*, p. 274

ability, to fill the gaps they leave. He is well pleased when they are appreciated; for they are links in His chain of service.

Men who are self-important, who are filled with the thought of their own superior abilities, overlook these humble, contrite workers; but not for one moment does God lose sight of them. He marks all that they do to help those in need of help. In the heavenly courts, when the redeemed are gathered home, they will stand nearest the Son of God. They will shine brightly in the courts of the Lord, honored by Him because they have felt it an honor to minister to those for whom He gave His life.[23]

The church on earth, united with the church in heaven, can accomplish all things.[24]

---

[23] *Testimonies for the Church*, vol. 7, pp. 25, 26
[24] *Testimonies for the Church*, vol. 7, p. 31

3

What Families Can Do

Missionary Families

Very much more might be done for Christ if all who have the light of truth would practice the truth. There are whole families who might be missionaries, engaging in personal labor, toiling for the Master with busy hands and active brains, devising new methods for the success of His work. There are earnest, prudent, warm-hearted men and women who could do much for Christ if they would give themselves to God, drawing near to Him, and seeking Him with the whole heart.

My brethren and sisters, take an active part in the work of soul-saving. This work will give life and vigor to the mental and spiritual powers. Light from Christ will shine into the mind. The Saviour will abide in your hearts, and in His light you will see light.

Can not be Done by Proxy

Consecrate yourselves wholly to the work of God. He is your strength, and He will be at your right hand, helping you to carry on His merciful designs. By personal labor reach those around you. Become acquainted with them. Preaching will not do the work that needs to be done. Angels of God attend you to the dwellings of those you visit. This work can not be done by proxy. Money lent or given will not accomplish it. Sermons will not do it. By visiting the people, talking, praying, sympathizing with them, you will win hearts. This is the highest missionary work that you can do. To do it, you will need resolute, persevering faith, unwearying patience, and a deep love for souls.

Find access to the people in whose neighborhood you live. As you tell them of the truth, use words of Christlike sympathy. Remember that the Lord Jesus is the Master-worker. He waters the seed sown. He puts into your minds words that will reach hearts. Expect that God will sustain the consecrated, unselfish worker. Obedience, childlike faith, trust in God, — these will bring peace and joy. Work disinterestedly, lovingly, patiently, for all with whom you are brought into contact. Show no impatience. Utter not one unkind word. Let the love of Christ be in your hearts, the law of kindness on your lips.

It is a mystery that there are not hundreds at work where now there is but one. The heavenly universe is astonished at the apathy, the coldness, the listlessness of those who profess to be sons and daughters of God. In the truth there is a living power. Go forth in faith, and proclaim the truth as if you believed it. Let those for whom you labor see that to you it is indeed a living reality.[25]

Relieve Physical Necessities

Christ's example must be followed by those who claim to be His children. Relieve the physical necessities of your fellow-men, and their gratitude will break down the barriers, and enable you to reach their hearts. Consider this matter earnestly. As churches, you have had opportunity to work as laborers together with God. Had you obeyed the word of God, had you entered upon this work, you would have been blessed and encouraged, and would have obtained a rich experience. You would have found yourselves, as the human agencies of God, earnestly advocating a scheme of saving, of restoration, of salvation. This scheme would not be fixed, but progressive, moving on from grace to grace, and from strength to strength.

The Lord has presented before me the work that is to be done in our cities. The believers in these cities are to work for God in the neighborhood of their homes. They are to labor quietly and in humility, carrying with them wherever they go the atmosphere of heaven. If they keep self out of sight, pointing always to Christ, the power of their influence will be felt.

It is not the Lord's purpose that ministers should be left to do the greatest part of the work of sowing the seeds of truth. Men who are not called to the ministry are to labor for their Master according to their several ability. As a worker gives himself unreservedly to the

---

[25] *Testimonies for the Church*, vol. 9, pp. 40 - 42

service of the Lord, he gains an experience that enables him to work more and more successfully for the Master. The influence that drew him to Christ helps him to draw others to Christ.[26]

Gospel Work for Women

Women as well as men can engage in the work of hiding the truth where it can work out and be made manifest. They can take their place in the work at this crisis, and the Lord will work through them. If they are imbued with a sense of their duty, and labor under the influence of the Spirit of God, they will have just the self-possession required for this time.

The Saviour will reflect upon these self-sacrificing women the light of His countenance, and this will give them a power that will exceed that of man. They can do in families a work that men can not do, a work that reaches the inner life They can come close to the hearts of those whom men can not reach. Their work is needed. Discreet and humble women can do a good work in explaining the truth to the people in their homes. The word of God thus explained will do its leavening work, and through its influence whole families will be converted.[27]

A Precious Experience for Our Sisters

Many of our sisters who bear the burden of home responsibilities have been willing to excuse themselves from undertaking any missionary work that requires thought and close application of mind; yet often this is the very discipline they need to enable them to perfect Christian experience. They may become workers for God by distributing to their neighbors tracts and papers that correctly represent our faith, and by sending these silent messengers through the mails to those who are willing to read and investigate. As they thus do what they can for others, they will gain many precious experiences.

My sisters, do not become weary in the distribution of our literature. This is a work you may all engage in successfully, if you are but connected with God. Before approaching your friends and neighbors, or writing letters of inquiry, lift the heart to God in prayer. All who with

---

[26] *Testimonies for the Church*, vol. 9, pp. 127, 128
[27] *Testimonies for the Church*, vol. 9, pp. 128, 129

humble heart take part in this work, will be educating themselves as acceptable workers in the vineyard of the Lord.

God Calls You

Let every sister who claims to be a child of God, feel a responsibility to help all within her reach. The noblest of all attainments may be gained through practical self-denial and benevolence, for others' good. Sisters, God calls you to work in the harvest field, and to help gather in the sheaves.[28]

Training Young Missionaries

The children should be educated in such a way that they will have sympathy for the aged and afflicted, and lend all the help in their power to alleviate the sufferings of the poor and distressed. They should be taught to be diligent in the missionary work; and from their earliest years, principles of self-denial and sacrifice for the good of others should be inculcated, that they may be laborers together with God.[29]

Will You Help

What is the great work before us? — The proclamation of the gospel, with its life-saving principles, to every nation and kindred and tongue and people. Let no one remain in idleness because he can not do the same class of work that the most experienced of God's servants are doing. Because you can not be in the highest place, will you do nothing? Because you can not trade upon pounds, will you refuse to trade upon the one pound? Because you have not five talents, will you put your one talent in a napkin and hide it in the earth? Because you can not work for the multitude, will you refuse to work for individuals? Do the smaller duties waiting for you. Thus you will help those who are bearing heavy responsibilities.

Use your talents, be they ever so few. God has certainly given you a work to do for Him. And in all you do, keep the Lord Jesus ever before you. Do all to the glory of His name. You belong to God, and you must do His work. Your life is sustained by the Giver of life. Your every capability, therefore, is to be put to use in His service. By using your

---

[28] *Review and Herald*, December 10, 1914
[29] *Testimonies for the Church*, vol. 6, p. 429

talents faithfully and wisely, you are gaining power to do better work, to bear heavier responsibilities.

Whatever you accomplish, be it little or much, leave it with God, remembering that it is not left for man to measure the work or the reward of his fellow-men. The Lord Jesus will give you the wages that are your due. Your reward will be in accordance with the spirit in which your work was done. Purity of motive, and earnest desire to glorify God, will bring to the earnest worker the same reward that comes to the one who accomplishes more. It is the principles by which the worker is governed that determine the reward.[30]

Recruits from Among the Children and the Uneducated

God will move upon men in humble positions to declare the message of present truth. Many such will be seen hastening hither and thither, constrained by the Spirit of God to give the light to those in darkness. The truth is as a fire in their bones, filling them with a burning desire to enlighten those who sit in darkness. Many, even among the uneducated, will proclaim the word of the Lord. Children will be impelled by the Holy Spirit to go forth to declare the message of heaven. The Spirit will be poured out upon those who yield to His promptings. Casting off man's binding rules and cautious movements, they will join the army of the Lord.[31]

Daily Opportunities for Seed Sowing

My brethren and sisters, study your plans; grasp every opportunity of speaking to your neighbors and associates, or of reading something to them from books that contain present truth. Show that you regard as of first importance the salvation of the souls for whom Christ has made so great a sacrifice.

In working for perishing souls, you have the companionship of angels. Thousands upon thousands, and ten thousand times ten thousand angels are waiting to co-operate with members of our churches in communicating the light that God has generously given, that a people may be prepared for the coming of Christ. "Now is the accepted time;

---

[30] *Australasian Union Conference Record*, February 15, 1904
[31] *Testimonies for the Church*, vol. 7, pp. 26, 27

behold, now is the day of salvation." Let every family seek the Lord in earnest prayer for help to do the work of God.

Do not pass by the little things, and look for a large work. You might do successfully the small work, but fail utterly in attempting a large work, and fall into discouragement. Take hold wherever you see that there is work to be done. Whether you are rich or poor, great or humble, God calls you into active service for Him. It will be by doing with your might what your hands find to do that you will develop talent and aptitude for the work. And it is by neglecting your daily opportunities that you become fruitless and withered. This is why there are so many fruitless trees in the garden of the Lord.

In the home circle, at your neighbor's fireside, at the bedside of the sick, in a quiet way you may read the Scriptures, and speak a word for Jesus and the truth. Precious seed may thus be sown that will spring up, and bring forth fruit after many days.[32]

Benefits of a Thorough Education

If placed under the control of His Spirit, the more thoroughly the intellect is cultivated, the more effectively it can be used in the service of God. The uneducated man who is consecrated to God and who longs to bless others can be, and is, used by the Lord in His service. But those who, with the same spirit of consecration, have had the benefit of a thorough education, can do a much more extensive work for Christ. They stand on vantage ground.

The Lord desires us to obtain all the education possible, with the object in view of imparting our knowledge to others. None can know where or how they may be called to labor or to speak for God. Our heavenly Father alone sees what He can make of men. There are before us possibilities which our feeble faith does not discern. Our minds should be so trained that if necessary we can present the truths of His word before the highest earthly authorities in such a way as to glorify His name. We should not let slip even one opportunity of qualifying ourselves intellectually to work for God.[33]

---

[32] *Testimonies for the Church*, vol. 9, pp. 129, 130
[33] *Christ's Object Lessons*, pp. 333, 334

The Lord's Army

The Lord will fit men and women—yes, and children, as He did Samuel—for His work, making them His messengers. He who never slumbers or sleeps watches over each worker, choosing his sphere of labor. All heaven is watching the warfare which, under apparently discouraging circumstances, God's servants are carrying on. New conquests are being achieved, new honors won, as the Lord's servants, rallying round the banner of their Redeemer, go forth to fight the good fight of faith. All the heavenly angels are at the service of the humble, believing people of God, and as the Lord's army of workers here below sing their songs of praise, the choir above joins with them in thanksgiving, ascribing praise to God and His Son.[34]

This World a Training School

This world is a training school for the higher school, this life a preparation for the life to come. Here we are to be prepared for entrance into the heavenly courts. Here we are to receive and believe and practice the truth, until we are made ready for a home with the saints in light.[35]

---

[34] *Testimonies for the Church*, vol. 7, p. 17
[35] *Testimonies for the Church*, vol. 8, p. 200

4

Lay Members as Pioneers

Waste Places in the Vineyard

In humble dependence upon God, families are to settle in the waste places of His vineyard. Consecrated men and women are needed to stand as fruit-bearing trees of righteousness in the desert places of the earth. As the reward of their self-sacrificing efforts to sow the seeds of truth, they will reap a rich harvest. As they visit family after family, opening the Scriptures to those in spiritual darkness, many hearts will be touched.

In fields where the conditions are so objectionable and disheartening that many workers refuse to go to them, most remarkable changes for the better may be brought about by the efforts of self-sacrificing lay members. These humble workers will accomplish much, because they put forth patient, persevering effort, not relying upon human power, but upon God, who gives them His favor. The amount of good that these workers accomplish will never be known in this world.[36]

A Call from a Mission Field

Written from Australia

To those who are looking for a place where they may work in the Lord's vineyard, we way, Come over and help us. Come prepared to practice self-denial, determined that you will not fail nor be discouraged. We can not pay your passage to this country, nor can we give you large wages. We can not carry you financially or spiritually; but if you will come to do a work for the Master, if you are willing to visit and labor for souls where they are, come, and we will co-operate with you as

---

[36] *Testimonies for the Church*, vol. 7, pp. 22, 23

long as you will co-operate with God. [This cry now goes up from many fields.]

Room for All

There is room in the work of God for all who are filled with the spirit of self-sacrifice. We have a solemn work before us. God is calling for men and women who are willing to experience travail of soul, men and women who are consecrated to His work. We need in this country, men who have a solid experience in the things of God, who, when they encounter difficulties, will hold firmly to the work, saying, We will not fail nor be discouraged. We want men who will strengthen and build up the work, not tear down and seek to destroy that which others are trying to do. We need men and women whom God can work, the fallow ground of whose hearts has been broken up.[37]

Giving Part Time to Neighborhood Ministry

Now I urge that more attention be given to eternal realities. Let every soul be aroused, and show that he appreciates the value of souls for whom Christ died. Let every one inquire, "What can I do to let the light shine forth to others?" Where is the missionary spirit? Where are those who will come to this part of the world and establish themselves in localities where they can lift the standard of truth, working in a quiet way? [Also written from australia.] Although they may not be able to give their whole time to the work, they can give a portion, they can exert a good and saving influence, and God will work through them.

Our field is the world, and we may all find ample room in which to work. But there is a great lack of money in the treasury, and if none shall engage in the work but men who are paid wages, what will become of the multitudes that are in darkness? Let all pray that the Lord will teach them how to use his gifts, to do their work with fidelity.[38]

Laymen Needed in New Fields

I wish there were men and women who could appreciate the situation, and would decide to move to these countries, Australia and New Zealand. Helpers are needed who have some means, who can engage

---

[37] *Manuscript Releases*, vol. 13, p. 397
[38] *Letter 23a, 1892*, September 25, 1892

in some employment and sustain themselves and not draw upon the Conference for their support. With genuine faith in the message of truth, such workers could settle in our cities as missionaries, letting their light shine forth to others.

It is not ordained ministers upon whom we must depend for this work, but laymen who love and fear God, and who feel the burden for the salvation of souls. They can be agents and co-workers with divine providence in seeking to save the lost. We want those who have sanctified energy, moral and intellectual. Let these put to use the talents they have, and by exercise they will grow. It can not be otherwise if they abide in Christ. In His companionship they will be constantly growing in wisdom. Christ says, "Without Me ye can do nothing." With Christ by your side, as your Teacher and Leader you can do all things.

There are many who have for years been rejoicing in the light of truth; let them now practice the lessons they have learned. They have the word of God, and the precious experience. Let them use the knowledge to a purpose. In all humility of mind seek to learn ways and methods of reaching those who are still in error and darkness. God calls; shall we hear His voice? God calls upon the lay members of His church to enter the field and do what they can by individual effort. All are to work for perishing souls, laying hold by faith upon the power of faith to work with them. Moments are precious.

Learning by Experience

Every one must be a learner, not a graduate; he must engage in the work with a humble heart, wholly dependent upon God. He may make mistakes, but errors in judgment will be corrected by education. Defeats may be turned to victories. As he advances, he can learn wisdom through failure, caution from imprudence. But learn, not let go. Keep the dear Saviour by your side; pray always; ask counsel of Jesus.

There are thousands who, if they would give themselves to the Lord without selfish reservation, might go with their families into new regions where the truth is not known, and establish themselves as citizens, and then watch for souls as they that must give an account. They might speak to the young, telling them of the love of Jesus. They could visit families, and in a pleasant manner introduce some excellent reading from our papers or publications. Let these silent messengers speak to them; and when the opportunities seem to be favorable, suggest a season of prayer, and the reading of the Bible. Angels of God will open ways for all such workers; they may become channels of light. Let them be constantly learning, constantly receiving, and constantly giving....

Hundreds of Humble Workers Needed

What is needed then, is to set at work scores, yes hundreds, who now have their light hidden under a bushel or under a bed....

There are souls who are willing to make any move for Christ's sake, but they think they are not qualified to do the sacred work of God. They have accepted the truth, and rejoice in it; but they have not come to the point to cry. "Speak, Lord; for Thy servant heareth." They do not seek to make terms with the Lord; if they are convinced that He calls them, they will make any and every sacrifice for the truth's sake. It is just such ones as these who are little in their own eyes, that the Lord chooses to use in the work of saving souls. They are not required to preach doctrinal discourses; but by personal effort they can reach hearts, and win them for Christ and the truth.

Willing to Sacrifice

Let such workers go into cities or other localities where the truth has not been introduced, or where it was presented years ago and the work has not been followed up. There are many places in cities and villages where these who have the light should set up the standard. True, it will require self-denial to leave the churches where they have assembled to worship God. But, if Jesus, the precious Saviour, had studied His own pleasure and convenience, as many who profess to be His followers do today, He would never have left the mansions of bliss, His heavenly home, and come to our world, all seared and marred with the curse....

Those who love God supremely and their fellow-men as themselves, will be ready to every good word and work. If they understand that the voice of God says, "Go," they do not stop to confer with flesh and blood, or allow their temporal, personal interest to block the way. They reason that Jesus gave himself to save their souls from ruin, and although they think it possible for them to do but little, they will do that heartily as to the Lord. They first give themselves, and they call not anything their own which they possess, whether it be aptitude, skill in any direction, learning, position, wealth or influence; they regard themselves as stewards of the manifold grace of God and servants for Christ's sake. It is such men and women that are Christ's witnesses. Their hearts throb in unison with His, their ears are quick to hear every Macedonian cry.[39]

Angels to Aid Us

Nothing is apparently more helpless, yet really more invincible, than the soul that feels its nothingness, and relies wholly on the merits of the Saviour. God would send every angel in heaven to the aid of such an one, rather than allow him to be overcome.[40]

A Call from the South

In the South there is much that could be done by lay members of the church, persons of limited education. There are men, women, and children who need to be taught to read. These poor souls are starving for a knowledge of God.

Our people in the South are not to wait for eloquent preachers, talented men; they are to take up the work which the Lord places before them, and do their best. He will accept and work through humble, earnest men and women, even though they may not be eloquent or highly educated. My brethren and sisters, devise wise plans for labor, and go forward, trusting in the Lord. Do not indulge the feeling that you are capable and keen-sighted. Begin and continue in humility. Be a living exposition of the truth. Make the word of God the man of your counsel. Then the truth will go with power, and souls will be converted.

Let Sabbath-keeping families move to the South, and live out the truth before those who know it not. These families can be a help to one another, but let them be careful to do nothing that will hedge up their way.

---

[39] *Letter 19b, 1892*, July 2, 1892
[40] *Testimonies for the Church*, vol. 7, p. 17

Christian Help Work Needed

Let them do Christian help work, feeding the hungry and clothing the naked. This will have a far stronger influence for good than the preaching of sermons. Deeds as well as words, of sympathy are needed. Christ prefaced the giving of His message by deeds of love and benevolence. Let these workers go from house to house, helping where help is needed, and, as opportunity offers, telling the story of the cross. Christ is to be their text. They need not dwell upon doctrinal subjects; let them speak of the work and sacrifice of Christ. Let them hold up His righteousness, in their lives revealing His purity. The true missionary must be armed with the mind of Christ. His heart must be filled with Christ-like love; and he must be true and steadfast to principle.

Establish Schools

In many places schools should be established, and those who are tender and sympathetic, who, like the Saviour, are touched by the sight of woe and suffering, should teach old and young. Let the word of God be taught in a way that will enable all to understand it. Let the pupils be encouraged to study the lessons of Christ. This will do more to enlarge the mind and strengthen the intellect than any other study. Nothing gives such vigor to the faculties as contact with the word of God.[41]

The Kind of Education to be Given

Where are the families who will become missionaries, and who will engage in labor in this field? Where are the men who have means and experience so that they can go forth to these people, and work for them just where they are? There are men who can educate them in agricultural lines, who can teach them to sow seed and plant orchards. There are others who can teach them to read, and can give them an object-lesson from their own life and example. Show them what you yourself can do to gain a livelihood, and it will be an education to them.[42]

---

[41] *Testimonies for the Church*, vol. 7, pp. 227, 228
[42] *The Southern Work*, pp. 23, 24

31

Encourage those Who are Willing to Work

Prepare workers to go out in the highways and hedges. We need wise nurserymen who will transplant trees to different localities, and give them advantages that they may grow....

Rally workers who possess true missionary zeal, and let them go forth to diffuse light and knowledge far and near. Let them take the living principles of health reform into the communities that to a large degree are ignorant of these principles.

There should be no delay in this work. Workers should be chosen who are fully consecrated, and who understand the sacredness and importance of the work. Do not send those who are not qualified in these respects. We want men who will push the triumphs of the cross; men who will persevere under discouragements and privations; men who will have the zeal and resolution and faith that are indispensable in the missionary field.

And to those who do not engage personally in the work, I would say, Do not hinder those who are willing to work; but give them your encouragement and support. After a time as the work advances, schools will be established in many cities, where workers can be quickly educated and trained for service.[43]

Not for Worldly Advantage

The lay members of our churches can accomplish a work which, as yet, they have scarcely begun. None should move into new places merely for the sake of worldly advantage; but where there is an opening to obtain a livelihood, let families that are well grounded in the truth enter, one or two families in a place, to work as missionaries. They should feel a love for souls, a burden of labor for them, and should make it a study how to bring them into the truth. They can distribute our publications, hold meetings in their homes, become acquainted with their neighbors, and invite them to come to these meetings. Thus they can let their light shine in good works.

---

[43] *Manuscript 11-1908*, February 15, 1908

Weeping, Praying, Laboring

Let the workers stand alone in God, weeping, praying, laboring for the salvation of their fellow-men. Remember that you are running a race, striving for a crown of immortality. While so many love the praise of men more than the favor of God, let it be yours to labor in humility. Learn to exercise faith in presenting your neighbors before the throne of grace, and pleading with God to touch their hearts. In this way effectual missionary work may be done. Some may be reached who would not listen to a minister or a colporteur. And those who thus labor in new places will learn the best ways of approaching the people, and can prepare the way for other laborers.[44]

Without Needed Facilities

Those who are endeavoring to build up the work in new territory will often find themselves in great need of better facilities. Their work will seem to be hindered for lack of these facilities; but let them not lose their faith and courage. Often they are obliged to go to the limit of their resources. At times it may seem as if they could advance no farther. But if they pray and work in faith. God will answer their petitions, sending them means for the advancement of the work. Difficulties will arise; they will wonder how they are going to accomplish what must be done. At times the future will look very dark. But let the workers bring to God the promises He has made, and thank Him for what He has done. Then the way will open before them, and they will be strengthened for the duty of the hour.[45]

Entire Self-Support Sometimes Impossible

Calls for workers are coming from all parts of the world. Means are called for to open new fields. Laborers need to be supported in many fields where it is impossible for them to be wholly self-supporting. While the needs of the world are making such demands upon us, our sanitariums will not be honoring God, if they indulge in any form of extravagance. They must work in Christ's lines.[46]

---

[44] *Testimonies for the Church*, vol. 8, p. 245
[45] *Gospel Workers*, pp. 267, 268
[46] *Letter 254-1907*, August 15, 1907

The Lord Will Prepare the Way

Angels who minister to those who shall be heirs of salvation, are saying to every true saint. There is work for you to do. "Go, stand and speak ... to the people the words of this life." If those addressed would obey this injunction, the Lord would prepare the way before them, putting them in possession of means whereby they could go.[47]

---

[47] *The Southern Worker*, October 10, 1899

5

An Unsalaried Ministry

Unsalaried Workers Needed

The burden of the work has been left largely with those who are laboring under salary. But this is not as it should be. The great missionary field is open to all, and the lay members of our churches must understand that no one is exempted from labor in the Master's vineyard.... [48]

Follow Me

When Christ called His disciples to follow Him, He offered them no flattering prospects in this life. He gave them no promise of gain or worldly honor, nor did they make any stipulation as to what they should receive. To Matthew as he sat at the receipt of custom, the Saviour said, "'Follow Me.' And he left all, rose up, and followed Him." Matthew did not, before rendering service, wait to demand a certain salary, equal to the amount received in his former occupation. Without question or hesitation he followed Jesus. It was enough for him that he was to be with the Saviour, that he might hear His words and unite with Him in His work.

So it was with the disciples previously called. When Jesus bade Peter and his companions follow Him, immediately they left their boats and nets. Some of these disciples had friends dependent on them for support; but when they received the Saviour's invitation, they did not hesitate, and inquire. "How shall I live, and sustain my family?" They were obedient to the call; and when afterward Jesus asked them, "When I sent you without purse, and scrip, and shoes, lacked ye anything?" they could answer, "Nothing."

---

[48] *The Review and Herald*, October 22, 1914

Today the Saviour calls us, as He called Matthew and John and Peter, to His work. If our hearts are touched by His love, the question of compensation will not be uppermost in our minds. We shall rejoice to be co-workers with Christ, and we shall not fear to trust His care. If we make God our strength, we shall have clear perceptions of duty, unselfish aspirations; our life will be actuated by a noble purpose, which will raise us above sordid motives.

God Will Provide

Many who profess to be Christ's followers have an anxious, troubled heart, because they are afraid to trust themselves with God. They do not make a complete surrender to Him, for they shrink from the consequences that such a surrender may involve. Unless they do make this surrender, they can not find peace.

There are many whose hearts are aching under a load of care because they seek to reach the world's standard. They have chosen its service, accepted its perplexities, adopted its customs. Thus their character is marred, and their life made a weariness. The continual worry is wearing out the life forces. Our Lord desires them to lay aside this yoke of bondage. He invites them to accept His yoke; He says, "My yoke is easy, and My burden is light." Worry is blind, and can not discern the future; but Jesus sees the end from the beginning. In every difficulty He has His way prepared to bring relief. "No good thing will He withhold from them that walk uprightly."

Our heavenly Father has a thousand ways to provide for us of which we know nothing. Those who accept the one principle of making the service of God supreme, will find perplexities vanish, and a plain path before their feet.

Encouraging Faith

The faithful discharge of today's duties is the best preparation for tomorrow's trials. Do not gather together all tomorrow's liabilities and cares and add them to the burden of today. "Sufficient unto the day is the evil thereof."

Let us be hopeful and courageous. Despondency in God's service is sinful and unreasonable. He knows our every necessity. To the omnipotence of the King of kings our covenant-keeping God unites the gentleness and care of the tender shepherd. His power is absolute, and it is the pledge of the sure fulfilment of His promises to all who trust in Him. He has means for the removal of every difficulty, that those who serve Him and respect the means He employs may be sustained. His love is as far above all other love as the heavens are above the earth. He watches over children with a love that is measureless and everlasting.

In the darkest days, when appearances seem most forbidding, have faith in God. He is working out His will doing all things well in behalf of His people. The strength of those who love and serve Him will be renewed day by day.

He is able and willing to bestow upon His servants all the help they need. He will give them the wisdom which their varied necessities demand.

Said the tried apostle Paul: "He said unto me. My grace is sufficient for thee; for My strength is made perfect in weakness. Most gladly therefore will I rather glory in my infirmities, that the power of Christ may rest upon me. Therefore I take pleasure in infirmities, in reproaches, in necessities, in persecutions, in distresses for Christ's sake: for when I am weak, then am I strong."[49]

Work Unselfishly

The whole church needs to be imbued with the missionary spirit; then there will be many to work unselfishly in various ways as they can, without being salaried. There is altogether too much dependence on machinery, on mechanical working. Machinery is good in its place, but do not allow it to become too complicated. I tell you that in many cases it has retarded the work, and kept out laborers who in their line could have accomplished far more than has been done by the minister who depends on sermonizing more than on ministry.

Young men need to catch the missionary spirit, to be thoroughly imbued with the spirit of the message. "Put ye on the Lord Jesus Christ, and make no provision for the flesh to fulfil the lusts thereof." Work in any capacity, work where God leads you, in the line best suited to your talents, and best adapted to reach classes that have hitherto been

---

[49] *The Ministry of Healing*, pp. 479 - 482

sadly neglected. This kind of labor will develop intellectual and moral power, and adaptability to the work....

Christians will manifest the self-sacrificing spirit of Christ in their work, in connection with every branch of the cause.... They will not, can not, live in luxury and self-indulgence, while there are suffering ones around them....

Let none of those who name the name of Christ be cowards in His cause. For Christ's sake stand as if looking within the open portals of the city of God.[50]

The Experience of Paul and Its Lessons

While Paul was careful to set before his converts the plain teaching of Scripture regarding the proper support of the work of God, and while he claimed for himself, as a minister of the gospel, the power to forbear working" at secular employment as a means of self-support, yet at various times during his ministry in the great centers of civilization, he wrought at a handicraft for his own maintenance.[51]

There were some who objected to Paul's toiling with his hands, declaring that it was inconsistent with the work of a gospel minister. Why should Paul, a minister of the highest rank, thus connect mechanical work with the preaching of the Word? Was not the laborer worthy of his hire? Why should he spend in making tents time that to all appearance could be put to better account?

An Example of Industry

But Paul did not regard as lost the time thus spent. As he worked with Aquila he kept in touch with the great Teacher, losing no opportunity of witnessing for the Saviour and of helping those who needed help. His mind was ever reaching out for spiritual knowledge. He gave his fellow-workers instruction in spiritual things, and he also set an example of industry and thoroughness. He was a quick, skillful worker, diligent in business, "fervent in spirit, serving the Lord." As he worked at his trade, the apostle had access to a class of people that he could not otherwise have reached. He showed his associates that skill in the common arts is a gift from God, who provides both the gift, and the

---

[50] *The Southern Work,* p. 17
[51] *The Acts of the Apostles,* p. 346

wisdom to use it aright. He taught that even in everyday toil, God is to be honored. His toil-hardened hands detracted nothing from the force of his pathetic appeals as a Christian minister.[52]

Not all who feel that they have been called to preach should be encouraged to throw themselves and their families at once upon the church for continuous financial support. ... Young men who desire to exercise their gifts in the work of the ministry, will find a helpful lesson in the example of Paul at Thessalonica, Corinth, Ephesus, and other places. Although an eloquent speaker, and chosen by God to do a special work, he was never above labor, nor did he ever weary of sacrificing for the cause he loved.[53]

An Inspiration to Humble Toilers

Paul set an example against the sentiment, then gaining influence in the church, that the gospel could be proclaimed successfully only by those who were wholly freed from the necessity of physical toil. He illustrated in a practical way what might be done by consecrated laymen in many places where the people were unacquainted with the truths of the gospel. His course inspired many humble toilers with a desire to do what they could to advance the cause of God, while at the same time they supported themselves in daily labor. Aquila and Priscilla were not called to give their whole time to the ministry of the gospel; yet these humble laborers were used by God to show Apollos the way of truth more perfectly. The Lord employs various instrumentalities for the accomplishment of His purpose; and while some with special talents are chosen to devote all their energies to the work of teaching and preaching the gospel, many others, upon whom human hands have never been laid in ordination, are called to act an important part in soul-saving.

There is a large field open before the self-supporting gospel worker. Many may gain valuable experience in ministry while toiling a portion of the time at some form of manual labor; and by this method strong workers may be developed for important service in needy fields.[54]

---

[52] *The Acts of the Apostles*, pp. 351, 352
[53] *The Acts of the Apostles*, p. 354
[54] *The Acts of the Apostles*, p. 355

Assisting His Fellow-Laborers

Paul sometimes worked night and day, not only for his own support, but that he might assist his fellow-laborers. He shared his earnings with Luke, and helped Timothy. He even suffered hunger at times, that he might relieve the necessities of others.[55]

"These hands," he declared. "have ministered unto my necessities, and to them that were with me." Amidst his arduous labors and extensive journeys for the cause of Christ, he was able, not only to supply his own wants, but to spare something for the support of his fellow-laborers and the relief of the worthy poor. This he accomplished only by unremitting diligence and the closest economy. Well might he point to his own example, as he said, "I have showed you all things, how that so laboring ye ought to support the weak and to remember the words of the Lord Jesus, how He said, 'It is more blessed to give than to receive.'"[56]

Conditions of Success

The Lord is well pleased when those who go forth as missionaries, are more anxious for the salvation of souls than they are regarding the wages they shall receive for their work. When Christ's witnesses work under the Holy Spirit's guidance, when they are stripped of all selfishness, souls are converted by their earnest, patient, persevering efforts.

In Poverty and Helplessness

Let two or more persons start out together in evangelistic work. They may not get any particular encouragement from those at the head of the work that they will be sustained but nevertheless, let them go forward, praying, singing, teaching living the truth. They may take up the important work of canvassing, and in this way introduce the truth into many families. As they move forward in their work, they gain a blessed experience. They are humbled by a sense of their poverty and helplessness, but the Lord manifestly goes before them.

Among the wealthy and the poor they find favor and help. They come close in friendship to those for whom they work, the one imparting the

---

[55] *The Acts of the Apostles*, p. 352
[56] *The Acts of the Apostles*, pp. 395, 396

treasures of the Word, the other imparting temporal sustenance, and both are blessed. Even the poverty of the workers is a means of finding access to the people. As these humble missionaries pass on their way they are helped in many ways by those to whom they bring spiritual food. Many isolated ones are brought to a knowledge of the truth, who, but for these humble teachers, would never have been won to Christ.

An Exhausted Treasury No Reason for Delay

Self-supporting missionaries are often very successful. Beginning in a small and humble way, their work enlarges under the guidance of the Spirit of God.

This work all can do who have received the truth into the heart. Providence opens the way for workers to go to isolated places, and if they bear the message God gives them, their efforts will be crowned with success.

God calls for men to enter the whitening harvest field. Shall His workmen wait because the treasury is exhausted, because there is scarcely enough to sustain the workers now in the field? Go forth in faith, and God will be with you. "He that goeth forth and weepeth, bearing precious seed, shall doubtless come again with rejoicing, bringing his sheaves with him." Psalm 126:6. Nothing is so successful as success. Let this be secured, and the work will move forward. New fields will be opened. Many souls will be won to the truth. What is needed is increased faith in God.[57]

Moneyed Men to Help

For years the perplexing question has been before us. How can we raise funds adequate for the support of the missions which the Lord has gone before us to open?... The Lord desires that moneyed men shall be converted, and act as His helping hand in reaching others. He desires that those who can help in the work of reform and restoration shall see the precious light of truth and be transformed in character, and led to use their entrusted capital in His service. He would have

---

[57] *Manuscript 54a-1901*, July 1, 1901

them invest the means He has lent them, in doing good, in opening the way for the gospel to be preached to all classes nigh and afar off....

The compassionate Redeemer bids His servants give to rich and poor the call to the supper. Go out into the highways and the hedges, and by your persevering, determined efforts, compel them to come in. Let ministers of the gospel take hold of these worldly moneyed men, and bring them to the banquet of truth that Christ has prepared for them.[58]

When the Poor Have Done Their Part

There are men of wealth who will accept the last message, if the right kind of labor is put forth. The Lord has made men his stewards, and has entrusted to them the means to carry forward his work. When the poor have done all they can to advance the cause, the Lord will bring in men of means to carry on the work.[59]

The truth spreads when living, workers commend it by personal effort, characterized by piety and the beauty of true holiness.[60]

---

[58] *Testimonies for the Church*, vol. 9, pp. 114, 115
[59] *Gospel Workers* (1892 ed.), p. 298
[60] *The Review and Herald*, October 22, 1914

6

Various Means of Support

Opportunities for Laborers of Varied Gifts

In connection with the proclamation of the message in large cities, there are many kinds of work to be done by laborers with varied gifts. Some are to labor in one way, some in another. The Lord desired that the cities shall be worked by the united efforts of laborers of different capabilities. All are to look to Jesus for direction, not depending on man for wisdom, lest they be led astray. As laborers together with God, they should seek to be in harmony with one another. There should be frequent councils, and earnest whole-hearted co-operation. Yet all are to look to Jesus for wisdom, not depending upon men alone for direction.[61]

Engaging in Business

How are the people to be warned in these countries, [written from Australia] is the question. What can be done to proclaim the message when we have so little means to work with, and so few workers.

If several families who could understand the situation would move to these countries and engage in some business in places where a few keeping the Sabbath, and do missionary work for Christ's sake, I know that by personal labor and holding a steady influence they could do much good. O that the Lord would stir up the minds of many in America to give themselves to this work! I have tried again and again to place the situation before our people in Battle Creek, but no one responds.

There are men in America, who with their industrious habits could make a good living and yet exert an influence to win souls to the truth.

---

[61] *Testimonies for the Church*, vol. 9, p. 109

I wish I could make some impression on hearts while we remain here that we might persuade them to come for Christ's sake, for the sake of perishing souls for whom Christ has died. We could counsel together, and set in operation plans that would not require a great outlay of means, and yet effect much good. Every one here who can work is at work, but there is so large a territory to be worked, so many that have not yet heard the first sound of the message of warning....

Sometimes I feel that I must never leave this field until families are settled here from America as missionaries, not ordained ministers, but workers in different lines.[62]

Missionaries as Industrial Educators

Missionaries will be much more influential among the people if they are able to teach the inexperienced how to labor according to the best methods and to produce the best results. They will thus be able to demonstrate that missionaries can become industrial educators; and this kind of instruction will be appreciated especially where means are limited. A much smaller fund will be required to sustain such missionaries, because, combined with their studies, they have put to the very best use their physical powers in practical labor; and wherever they may go, all they have gained in this line will give them vantage ground.[63]

A Strong Spiritual Nerve Required

The skill with which the carpenter uses his tools, the strength with which the blacksmith makes the anvil ring come from God. Whatever we do, wherever we are placed. He desires to control our minds, that we do perfect work.... The essential lesson of contented industry in the necessary duties of life is yet to be learned by many of Christ's followers. It requires more grace, more stern discipline of character, to work for God in the capacity of mechanic, merchant, lawyer, or farmer, carrying the precepts of Christianity into the ordinary business of life, than to labor as an acknowledged missionary in the open field. It requires a strong spiritual nerve to bring religion into the workshop and the business office, sanctifying the details of everyday life, and

---

[62] *Letter 47-1892*, December 22, 1892
[63] *Testimonies for the Church*, vol. 6, pp. 176, 177

ordering every transaction according to to the standards of God's word. But this is what the Lord requires.[64]

A Work for Christian Farmers

Christian farmers can do real missionary work in helping the poor to find homes on the land, and in teaching them how to till the soil and make it productive. Teach them how to use the implements of agriculture, how to cultivate various crops, how to plant and care for orchards.

Many who till the soil fail to secure adequate returns because of their neglect. Their orchards are not properly cared for, the crops are not put in at the right time, and a mere surface work is done in cultivating the soil. Their ill success they charge to the unproductiveness of the land. False witness is often borne in condemning land that, if properly worked, would yield rich returns. The narrow plans, the little strength put forth, the little study as to the best methods, call loudly for reform.

Let proper methods be taught to all who are willing to learn. If any do not wish you to speak to them of advanced ideas, let the lessons be given silently. Keep up the culture of your own land. Drop a word to your neighbors when you can, and let the harvest be eloquent in favor of right methods. Demonstrate what can be done with the land when properly worked.[65]

Move Forward Courageously

He who taught Adam and Eve in Eden how to tend the garden, desires to instruct men today. There is wisdom for him who drives the plow and sows the seed. Before those who trust and obey Him, God will open ways of advance. Let them move forward courageously, trusting to Him to supply their needs according to the riches of His goodness.

He who fed the multitude with five loaves and two small fishes is able today to give us the fruit of our labor. He who said to the fishers of Galilee, "Let down your nets for a draught," and who, as they obeyed, filled their nets till they broke, desires His people to see in this an evidence of what He will do for them today.

---

[64] *Counsels to Parents, Teachers, and Students*, pp. 277 - 279
[65] *The Ministry of Healing*, p. 193

The God who in the wilderness gave the children of Israel manna from heaven still lives and reigns. He will guide His people, and give skill and understanding in the work they are called to do. He will give wisdom to those who strive to do their duty conscientiously and intelligently. He who owns the world is rich in resources, and will bless every one who is seeking to bless others.

We need to look heavenward in faith. We are not to be discouraged because of apparent failure, nor should we be disheartened by delay. We should work cheerfully, hopefully, gratefully, believing that the earth holds in her bosom rich treasures for the faithful worker to garner, stores richer than gold or silver. The mountains and hills are changing; the earth is waxing old like a garment; but the blessing of God, which spreads for His people a table in the wilderness will never cease.[66]

Many are unwilling to earn their bread by the sweat of their brow, and they refuse to till the soil. But the earth has blessings hidden in her depths for those who have courage and will and perseverance to gather her treasures. Fathers and mothers who possess a piece of land and a comfortable home are kings and queens.[67]

Establishment of Industries as a Missionary Project

Attention should be given to the establishment of various industries so that poor families can find employment. Carpenters, blacksmiths, and indeed every one who understands some line of useful labor, should feel a responsibility to teach and help the ignorant and the unemployed.

In ministry to the poor there is a wide field of service for women as well as for men. The efficient cook, the housekeeper, the seamstress, the nurse, — the help of all is needed. Let the members of poor households be taught how to cook how to make and mend their own clothing, how to nurse the sick, how to properly care for the home. Let boys and girls be thoroughly taught some useful trade or occupation.[68]

---

[66] *The Ministry of Healing*, p. 200
[67] *Fundamentals of Christian Education*, p. 327
[68] *The Ministry of Healing*, p. 194

47

Small Sanitariums and Treatment Rooms

Today the truth is to be proclaimed as Christ proclaimed it when He was on this earth. Our people who are collected together at large centers should be out in the field working for souls. They should go to places where the truth has not yet been heard, and pray and plan and work and gain an experience by practical work. Is not Christ in our world today as verily as He was then? Can He not heal the sick as well now as then? Let small sanitariums and treatment rooms be established, and let people be given an education in the simple methods of treating disease. Those who take up this work will increase in capability; for unseen heavenly agencies will be present to help them.[69]

Beginning Work as Medical Missionaries

Men and women are to study how they can best reach the people. Then let them go forth as consecrated, spiritual workers. Let them in some city hire a place in which to live, and at once begin their work. They will find enough suffering ones to whom they can present themselves as medical missionaries. In some places the medical missionary will be better received if he has credentials to show that he has been set apart for gospel work.[70]

House-to-house Work

In many states there are settlements of industrious, well-to-do farmers, who have never had the truth for this time. Such places should be worked. Let our lay members take up this line of service. By lending or selling books, by distributing papers, and by holding Bible readings, our lay members could do much in their own neighborhoods. Filled with love for souls, they could proclaim the message with such power that many would be converted.

A Representation of What May Be Done

Two Bible workers were seated in a family. With the open Bible before them, they presented the Lord Jesus Christ as the sin-pardoning Saviour. Earnest prayer was offered to God, and hearts were softened and subdued by the influence of the Spirit of God. Their prayers were

---

[69] *Letter 43-1905*, January 29,1905
[70] *Manuscript 33-1901*, April 19, 1901

uttered with freshness and power. As the word of God was explained, I saw that a soft, radiant light illumined the Scriptures, and I said, softly, "Go out into, the highways and hedges, and compel them to come in, that My house may be filled." Luke 14:23.

The precious light was communicated from neighbor to neighbor. Family altars which had been broken down were again erected, and many were converted.

My brethren and sisters, give yourselves to the Lord for service. Allow no opportunity to pass unimproved. Visit the sick and suffering, and show a kindly interest in them. If possible, do something to make them more comfortable. Through this means you can reach their hearts, and speak a word for Christ.

Eternity alone will reveal how far-reaching such a line of labor can be. Other lines of usefulness will open before those who are willing to do the duty nearest them. It is not learned, eloquent speakers that are needed now, but humble. Christ-like men and women, who have learned from Jesus of Nazareth to be meek and lowly, and who, trusting in His strength, will go forth into the highways and hedges to give the invitation, "Come; for all things are now ready." Luke 14:17.

Use Varied Industries and Crafts

Those who are wise in agricultural lines, in tilling the soil, those who can construct simple, plain buildings, may help. They can do good work, and at the same time show in their characters the high standard to which it is the privilege of this people to attain. Let farmers, financiers, builders, and those who are skilled in various other crafts, go to neglected fields, to improve the land, to establish industries, to prepare humble homes for themselves, and to give their neighbors a knowledge of the truth for this time.[71]

Jesus does not release us from the necessity of effort, but He teaches that we are to make Him first and last and best in everything. We are to engage in no business, follow no pursuit, seek no pleasure, that would hinder the outworking of His righteousness in our character and life. Whatever we do is to be done heartily, as unto the Lord.[72]

---

[71] *Testimonies for the Church*, vol. 9, pp. 35, 36
[72] *Thoughts from the Mount of Blessing*, p. 111

Manufacture of Health Foods

Wherever the truth is proclaimed, instruction should be given in the preparation of healthful foods. God desires that in every place the people shall be taught to use wisely the products that can be easily obtained. Skilful teachers should show the people how to utilize to the very best advantage the products that they can raise or secure in their section of the country. Thus, the poor, as well as those in better circumstances, can learn to live healthfully.... Our work is to show the people how they can obtain and prepare the most wholesome food, how they can co-operate with God in restoring His moral image in themselves....

He who in the building of the tabernacle gave skill and understanding in all manner of cunning work, will give skill and understanding to His people in the combining of natural-food products, thus showing them how to secure a healthful diet....

It is the Lord's design that in every place men and women shall be encouraged to develop their talents by preparing healthful foods from the natural products of their own section of the country. If they look to God, exercising their skill and ingenuity under the guidance of His Spirit, they will learn how to prepare natural products into healthful foods. Thus they will be able to teach the poor how to provide themselves with foods that will take the place of flesh meat. Those thus helped can in turn instruct others.[73]

Restaurants

Wherever medical missionary work is carried on in our large cities, cooking-schools should be held; and wherever a strong educational missionary work is in progress, a hygienic restaurant of some sort should be established, which shall give a practical illustration of the proper selection and the healthful preparation of foods.[74]

A Means of Creating Interest

When the question of establishing restaurants was first introduced, it was clearly pointed out that the one aim and object of their work was to be the conversion of souls. It was not that you might invent the

[73] *Testimonies for the Church*, vol. 7, pp. 132, 133
[74] *Testimonies for the Church*, vol. 7, p. 55

many fancy dishes to gratify the appetite, and have no time left to devote to the work of creating in the minds of others an interest in the truth. Some attempts may have been made to interest souls in the truth, but they have been but feeble in comparison with what should have been done.[75]

Financial Aspect Not to Be All-absorbing

Our restaurants bring us in contact with many people, but if we allow our minds to be engrossed with the thought of financial profit, we shall fail to fulfil the purpose of God. He would have us to take advantage of every opportunity to present the truth that is to save men and women from eternal death.[76]

To Awaken Inquiry

When thinking men find that our restaurants are closed on the Sabbath, they will begin to make inquiries in regard to the principles that lead us to close our doors on Saturday. In answering their questions, we shall have opportunity to acquaint them with the truth. We can give them copies of our periodicals and tracts, so that they may be able to understand the difference between God's people and the so-called Christian world.[77]

Qualifying for the Work

Let all set their hearts and minds to become intelligent in regard to the work for this time, qualifying themselves to do that for which they are best adapted. Men who make a success in business life are keen, apt, and prompt. We must exercise equal tact and energy in the service of God. Let every man of whatever trade or profession, make the cause of God his first interest, not only exercising his talents to advance the Lord's work, but cultivating his ability to this end. Many a man devotes months and years to the acquirement of a trade or profession, that he may become a successful worker in the world. Should he not make as great an effort to cultivate those talents which would make him a successful worker for God? All this work of training should be accompanied with earnest seeking of the Lord for His Holy Spirit....

---

[75] *Manuscript Releases*, vol 8, p. 175
[76] *Welfare Ministry*, p. 286
[77] *Manuscript 108-1902*, August 7, 1902

Scriptural Knowledge Essential

There is a great neglect to obtain that scriptural knowledge which is essential, that the life in all points may be conformed to the spirit of the gospel. Very much has been lost by our unlikeness to Jesus, — lost because we do not in our own conduct present the loveliness of a Christ-like life, and adorn by the Christian graces the doctrine of our Saviour.[78]

As the Servants of Christ

Whatever work we do, we are to do it for Christ. There are many kinds of temporal work to be done for God. An unbeliever would do this work mechanically, for the wages he receives. He does not know the joy of co-operation with the Master Worker. There is no spirituality in the work of him who serves self. Common motives, common aspirations, common inspirations, a desire to be thought clever by men, rule in his life. Such a one may receive praise from men, but not from God. Those who are truly united with Christ do not work for the wages they receive. Laborers together with God, they do not strive to exalt self.

In the last great day decisions will be made that will be a surprise to many. Human judgment will have no place in the decisions then made. Christ can and will judge every case; for all judgment has been committed to Him by the Father. He will estimate service by that which is invisible to men. The most secret things lie open to His all-seeing eye. When the Judge of all men shall make His investigation, many of those whom human estimation has placed first will be placed last, and those who have been put in the lowest place by men will be taken out of the ranks and made first.[79]

---

[78] *The Review and Herald*, November 26, 1914
[79] *The Review and Herald*, July 31, 1900

7

Encourage the Self-Supporting Workers

Many Waiting to Commence Work

There are many who with proper encouragement would begin in out-of-the-way places to make efforts to seek and to save that which is lost. The Lord blesses these self-sacrificing ones, who have such a hunger for souls that they are willing to go anywhere to work. But in the past how much encouragement has been given to such workers by their brethren? Many of them have waited long for something to do, but no attention has been given to them.

If the ministers had given help and encouragement to these men and women, they would have been doing the work appointed them by the Lord. Some have seen the spiritual poverty of unworked fields, and have longed to do something to help. But it has taken so long for encouragement to come to them that many have gone into other lines of work.

The Macedonian cry is coming from every quarter. Shall men go to the regular lines to see whether they will be permitted to labor, or shall they go out and work as best they can, depending on their own abilities and on the help of the Lord, beginning in a humble way and creating an interest in the truth in places in which nothing has been done to give the warning message.

The Lord has encouraged those who have started out on their own responsibility to work for him, their hearts filled with love for souls ready to perish. A true missionary spirit will be imparted to those who seek earnestly to know God and Jesus Christ, whom He hath sent. The Lord lives and reigns. Young men, go forth into the places to which you are directed by the Spirit of the Lord. Work with your hands, that you may be self-supporting, and as you have opportunity proclaim the message of warning.[80]

In Union There is Strength

If Christians were to act in concert, moving forward as one, under the direction of one Power, for the accomplishment of one purpose, they would move the world.[81]

A Self-sacrificing Ministry

Many fields ripe for the harvest have not yet been entered, because of our lack of self-sacrificing helpers. These fields must be entered, and many laborers should go to them with the expectation of bearing their own expenses. But some of our ministers are little disposed to take upon them the burden of this work, little disposed to labor with the whole-hearted benevolence that characterized the life of our Lord.

God is grieved as He sees the lack of self-denial and perseverance in His servants. Angels are amazed at the spectacle. Let workers for Christ study His life of self-sacrifice. He is our example. Can the ministers of today expect to be called on to endure less hardship that did the early Christians, the Waldenses, and reformers in every age, in their efforts to carry the gospel to every land?

God has entrusted to His ministers the work of proclaiming His last message of mercy to the world. He is displeased with those who do not throw their whole energies into this all-important work. Unfaithfulness on the part of the appointed watchmen on the walls of Zion endangers the cause of truth, and exposes it to the ridicule of the enemy. It is time for our ministers to understand the responsibility and sacredness of their mission.[82]

Carry the Work Quickly

This is no time to colonize. From city to city, the work is to be carried quickly. The light that has been placed under a bushel is to be taken out and placed on a candlestick, that it may give forth light to all that are in the house.... Can we now depend upon our men in positions of responsibility to act humbly and nobly their part? Let the watchmen

---

[80] *Spaulding and Magan Collection*, p. 176
[81] *Testimonies for the Church*, vol. 9, p. 221
[82] *Testimonies for the Church*, vol. 7, p. 245

arouse. Let no one continue to be indifferent to the situation. There should be a thorough awakening among the brethren and sisters in all our churches....

Let companies now be quickly organized to go out two and two, and labor in the Spirit of Christ, following His plans. Even though some Judas may introduce himself into the ranks of the workers, the Lord will care for the work. His angels will go before and prepare the way. Before this time, every large city should have heard the testing message, and thousands should have been brought to a knowledge of the truth. Wake up the churches, take the light from under the bushel.[83]

Danger of Circumscribing the Work

The solemn and momentous work for this time is not to be carried forward to completion solely by the efforts of a few chosen men who have heretofore borne the responsibilities in the cause. When those whom God has called to aid in the accomplishment of a certain work shall have carried it as far as they can, with the ability he has given them, the Lord will not allow the work to stop at that stage. In His providence He will call and qualify others to unite with the first, that together they may advance still, farther, and lift the standard higher.

But there are some minds that do not grow with the work: instead of adapting themselves to its increasing demands, they allow it to extend far beyond them, and thus they find themselves unable to comprehend or to meet the exigencies of the times. When men whom God is qualifying to bear responsibilities in the cause, take hold of it in a slightly different way from that in which it has hitherto been conducted, the older laborers should be careful that their course be not such as to hinder these helpers or to circumscribe the work. Some may not realize the importance of certain measures, simply because they do not see the necessities of the work in all its bearings, and do not themselves feel the burden which God has specially laid upon other men. Those who are not specially qualified to do a certain work,

[83] *Medical Ministry,* pp. 302, 303

should beware that they do not stand in the way of others, and prevent them from fulfilling the purpose of God.[84]

No One Authorized to Hinder

In the future, men in the common walks of life will be impressed by the Spirit of the Lord to leave their ordinary employment, and go forth to proclaim the last message of mercy. As rapidly as possible they are to be prepared for labor, that success may crown their efforts. They co-operate with heavenly agencies; for they are willing to spend and be spent in the service of the Master. No one is authorized to hinder these workers. They are to be bidden Godspeed as they go forth to fulfil the great commission. No taunting word is to be spoken of them as in the rough places of the earth they sow the gospel seed.

Life's best things, — simplicity, honesty, truthfulness purity, unsullied integrity, — can not be bought or sold; they are as free to the ignorant as to the educated, to the black man as to the white man, to the humble peasant as to the king upon his throne. Humble workers, who do not trust in their own strength, but who labor in simplicity, trusting always in God, will share in the joy of the Saviour. Their persevering prayers will bring souls to the cross. In co-operation with their self-sacrificing efforts, Jesus will move upon hearts, working miracles in the conversion of souls. Men and women will be gathered into church fellowship. Meeting-houses will be built, and schools established. The hearts of the workers will be filled with joy as they see the salvation of God.[85]

Be Slow to Criticize the Methods of Others

Some workers pull with all the power that God has given them, but they have not yet learned that they should not pull alone. Instead of isolating themselves, let them draw in harmony with their fellow-laborers. Unless they do this, their activity will work at the wrong time and in the wrong way. They will often work counter to that which God would have done, and thus their work is worse than wasted.

On the other hand, the leaders among God's people are to guard against the danger of condemning the methods of individual workers

---

[84] *Testimonies for the Church*, vol. 5, p. 722
[85] *Testimonies for the Church*, vol. 7, pp. 27, 28

who are led by the Lord to do a special work that but few are fitted to do. Let brethren in responsibility be slow to criticize movements that are not in perfect harmony with their methods of labor. Let them never suppose that every plan should reflect their own personality. Let them not fear to trust another's methods; for by withholding their confidence from a brother laborer who, with humility and consecrated zeal, is doing a special work in God's appointed way, they are retarding the advancement of the Lord's cause.

Avoid Distrustful Caution

God can and will use those who have not had a thorough education in the schools of men. A doubt of His power to do this, is manifest unbelief; it is limiting the omnipotent power of the One with whom nothing is impossible. O, for less of this uncalled-for distrustful caution! It leaves so many forces of the church unused; it closes up the way, so that the Holy Spirit can not use men; it keeps in idleness those who are willing and anxious to labor in Christ's lines; it discourages from entering the work many who would become efficient laborers together with God, if they were given a fair chance.[86]

A Blessing to Those Who Follow God's Plan

Let no man think that because a fellow-worker does not follow his ideas and plans, he can not be doing right. When a man thinks this, he exerts an influence which hinders God by hindering the one through whom He is working. It is God's purpose that the world shall receive the truth through the spoken and written word. His servants are to use their varied gifts in the gospel ministry, and they are to be assisted by the printed page. This is the plan which the Lord has ordained. As it is carried out in accordance with His direction the truth will go forth as a lamp that burneth.

Through God's appointed agencies, His blessing is to come to the world. Those who will respect His word and follow His plan will see of His salvation.[87]

---

[86] *Testimonies for the Church*, vol. 9, pp. 258, 259
[87] *Manuscript 117-1901*, November 14, 1901

A Perfect Whole

While extensive plans should be laid, great care must be taken that the work in each branch of the cause be harmoniously united with that in every other branch, thus making a perfect whole.[88]

---

[88] *Testimonies for the Church*, vol. 9, p. 136

Bibliography

White, Ellen G. *Counsels to Parents, Teachers, and Students.* Mountain View, CA: Pacific Press Publishing Association, 1913.

White, Ellen G. *Fundamentals of Christian Education.* Nashville, TN: Southern Publishing Association, 1923.

White, Ellen G. *Gospel Workers.* Washington, DC: Review and Herald Publishing Association, 1915.

White, Ellen G. *Letter 47-1892, December 22, 1892*

White, Ellen G. *Letter 66-1902*, April 24, 1902.

White, Ellen G. *Life Sketches of Ellen G. White.* Mountain View, CA: Pacific Press Publishing Association, 1915.

White, Ellen G. *Manuscript 33-1901*, April 19, 1901

White, Ellen G. *Manuscript 54a-1901*, July 1, 1901.

White, Ellen G. *Manuscript 108-1902*, August 7, 1902.

White, Ellen G. *Manuscript 117-1901*, November 14, 1901.

White, Ellen G. *Manuscript 127-1901*, November 26, 1901.

White, Ellen G. *Manuscript Releases.* Vol. 8. Silver Spring, MD: Ellen G. White Estate, 1990.

White, Ellen G. *Medical Ministry.* Mountain View, CA: Pacific Press Publishing Association, 1932.

White, Ellen G. *The Ministry of Healing.* Mountain View, CA: Pacific Press Publishing Association, 1905.

White, Ellen G. *Spalding and Magan Collection.* Payson, AZ: Leaves-Of-Autumn Books, 1985.

White, Ellen G. *Testimonies for the Church.* Vol. 5. Mountain View, CA: Pacific Press Publishing Association, 1889.

White, Ellen G. *Testimonies for the Church.* Vol. 6. Mountain View, CA: Pacific Press Publishing Association, 1901.

White, Ellen G. *Testimonies for the Church.* Vol. 7. Mountain View, CA: Pacific Press Publishing Association, 1902.

White, Ellen G. *Testimonies for the Church*. Vol. 8. Mountain View, CA: Pacific Press Publishing Association, 1904.

White, Ellen G. *Testimonies for the Church*. Vol. 9. Mountain View, CA: Pacific Press Publishing Association, 1909.

White, Ellen G. *Thoughts from the Mount of Blessing*. Mountain View, CA: Pacific Press Publishing Association, 1896.

White, Ellen G. *Welfare Ministry*. Washington, DC: Review and Herald Publishing Association, 1952.

Australasia Union Conference Record, March 18, 1907.

The Review and Herald, January 17, 1893.

The Review and Herald, July 31, 1900.

The Review and Herald, October 22, 1914.

The Review and Herald, November 26, 1914.

The Southern Worker, October 10, 1899.

TEACH Services, Inc.
P U B L I S H I N G

We invite you to view the complete
selection of titles we publish at:
www.TEACHServices.com

We encourage you to write us
with your thoughts about this,
or any other book we publish at:
info@TEACHServices.com

TEACH Services' titles may be purchased in
bulk quantities for educational, fund-raising,
business, or promotional use.
bulksales@TEACHServices.com

Finally, if you are interested in seeing
your own book in print, please contact us at:
publishing@TEACHServices.com
We are happy to review your manuscript at no charge.